Bridging Grades

1 to 2 Summer Bridge ACTIVITIES
QUICK

#1 Teacher Recommended!

Carson Dellosa Education
Greensboro, North Carolina

Caution: Before beginning any food activity, ask parents' permission and inquire about the child's food allergies and religious or other food restrictions.

Caution: Before completing any balloon activity, ask parents' permission and inquire about possible latex allergies. Also, remember that uninflated or popped balloons may present a choking hazard.

Caution: Exercise activities may require adult supervision. Before beginning any exercise activity, consult a physician. Written parental permission is suggested for those using this book in group situations. Children should always warm up prior to beginning any exercise activity and should stop immediately if they feel any discomfort during exercise.

Caution: Nature activities may require adult supervision. Before beginning any nature activity, ask parents' permission and inquire about the child's plant and animal allergies. Remind the child not to touch plants or animals during the activity without adult supervision.

The authors and publisher are not responsible or liable for any injury that may result from performing the exercises or activities in this book.

Summer Bridge®
An imprint of Carson Dellosa Education
PO Box 35665
Greensboro, NC 27425 USA

© 2021 Carson Dellosa Education. Except as permitted under the United States Copyright Act, no part of this publication may be reproduced, stored, or distributed in any form or by any means (mechanically, electronically, recording, etc.) without the prior written consent of Carson Dellosa Education.

Printed in the USA • All rights reserved.   ISBN 978-1-4838-6279-8

02-059221151

Table of Contents

Making the Most of *Summer Bridge Activities® Quick* 4

Section I

Introduction to Flexibility 5
Activity Pages 6
Outdoor Extension Activities 16
Activity Pages 18
Outdoor Extension Activity 28

Section II

Introduction to Strength 29
Activity Pages 30
Outdoor Extension Activities 40
Activity Pages 42
Outdoor Extension Activity 52

Section III

Introduction to Endurance 53
Activity Pages 54
Outdoor Extension Activities 64
Activity Pages 66
Outdoor Extension Activity 76

Answer Key 77

Making the Most of *Summer Bridge Activities*® Quick

This book will help your child review first grade skills and preview second grade skills. Inside, find lots of resources that encourage your child to practice, learn, and grow while getting a head start on the new school year.

Just One Page a Day
...is all it takes to stay sharp with learning activities for each weekday, all summer long!

Month-by-Month Organization
Three color-coded sections match the three months of summer vacation. Each month begins with an introduction to the section's fitness and character-building focus.

Daily Activities
One page of activities is provided for each weekday. Activities cover math, reading comprehension, writing, grammar, science, and social studies.

Special Features

FITNESS FLASH: Quick exercises to develop strength, flexibility, and fitness

CHARACTER CHECK: Ideas for developing kindness, honesty, tolerance, and more

FACTOID: Fun trivia facts

Take It Outside! Fun activities for outdoor observation, exploration, learning, and play are scattered throughout each summer month.

Star Stickers: Use the star stickers at the back of the book. Place a sticker in the space provided at the end of each day's learning activities when the page is complete.

Monthly Goals

A *goal* is something that you want to accomplish. Sometimes, reaching a goal can be hard work! Think of three goals that you would like to set for yourself this month. Have an adult help you write your goals on the lines. Place a sticker next to each of your goals that you complete.

1. _____ [PLACE STICKER HERE]

2. _____ [PLACE STICKER HERE]

3. _____ [PLACE STICKER HERE]

Introduction to Flexibility

This section includes fitness and character development activities that focus on flexibility. If your child has limited mobility, feel free to modify any suggested exercises to fit their individual abilities.

Physical Flexibility

Flexibility, to the average person, means being able to accomplish everyday physical tasks easily, like bending to tie a shoe. Proper stretching allows muscles and joints to move through their full range of motion, which is key to maintaining good flexibility.

There are many ways that your child stretches every day without realizing it. Point out examples, such as reaching for a dropped pencil, and explain why good flexibility is important. Encourage them to set a stretching goal for the summer.

Flexibility of Character

It is also important to be mentally flexible. Mental flexibility means being open minded. Your child can practice mental flexibility by respecting the differences of other children, sharing, and taking turns.

Talk to your child about how disappointing it can be when things do not go their way and explain that disappointment is a normal reaction. Give a recent example of when unforeseen circumstances ruined plans. By using relatable examples, you can arm your child with tools to be flexible, such as having realistic expectations, brainstorming solutions to make a disappointing situation better, and looking for good things that may have resulted from the initial disappointment. Encourage your child to be flexible and praise them when you see them exhibiting this trait.

DAY 1  Handwriting/Phonics

Write the capital letters of the alphabet.

AB

Say the name of each picture. Write the vowel that completes each word.

1.  m____p	2.  c____t	3.  b____d
4.  c____p	5. 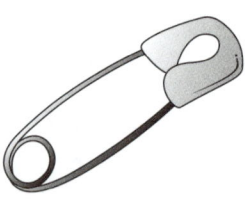 p____n	6.  t____p

FACTOID: The largest type of frog is the goliath frog. It can reach up to 12.5 inches (about 32 cm) in length.

Addition & Subtraction/Time DAY 2

Solve each problem.

1. 15 −11	2. 16 − 4	3. 13 − 8	4. 13 + 5	5. 19 − 3	6. 18 + 2
7. 8 +9	8. 17 − 9	9. 18 − 4	10. 12 + 6	11. 17 − 4	12. 15 + 4

Write the correct time for each clock that has hands. Draw hands on each clock that has a time below it.

13.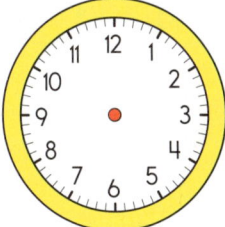
9:00

14.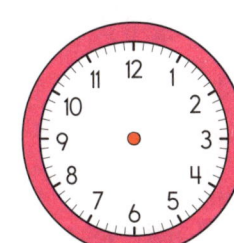
4:00

15.
___:___

16.
8:00

17.
___:___

18.
11:00

DAY 3

Handwriting/Reading Comprehension

Write the lowercase letters of the alphabet.

a b

Read each sentence. Draw a picture of your favorite sentence.

1. The cat sat on Alfonso's lap.

   The cat plays with the ball.

   The boy has a pet frog.

   The frog hops on Sam's bed.

   The man sat on his hat.

 **FITNESS FLASH:** Touch your toes 10 times.

* See page 2.

Geometry/Subtraction **DAY 4**

Follow the directions to color each shape.

1.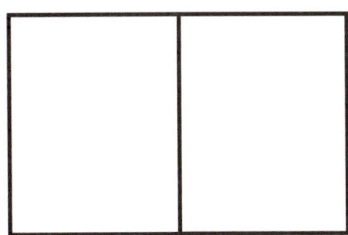
2.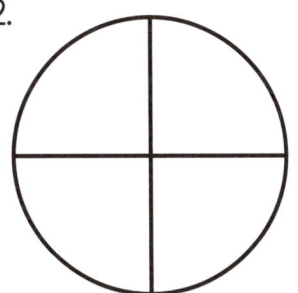
3.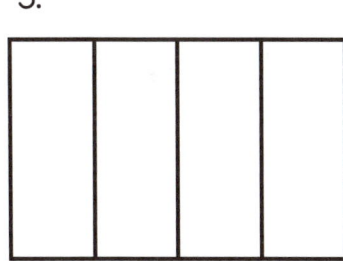

Color one half of the rectangle.

Color one quarter of the circle.

Color two fourths of the rectangle.

Follow the directions to solve each problem.

4. Start with 80. Write the number that is 60 less. _____

5. Start with 90. Write the number that is 40 less. _____

6. Start with 20. Write the number that is 10 less. _____

7. Start with 70. Write the number that is 50 less. _____

8. Start with 60. Write the number that is 30 less. _____

9. Start with 50. Write the number that is 10 less. _____

FITNESS FLASH: Do arm circles for 30 seconds.

* See page 2.

DAY 5

Language Arts & Grammar/Phonics

Add endings to write new words for each base word. (Hint: You may need to add an extra letter before the ending in some words.)

Base Word	Add -ed	Add -ing
jump	_____	_____
pat	_____	_____
open	_____	_____
start	_____	_____
touch	_____	_____
blink	_____	_____

Say the name of each picture. Write the letter of each long vowel sound.

1.
   ___

2.
   ___

3.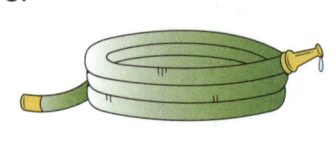
   ___

4.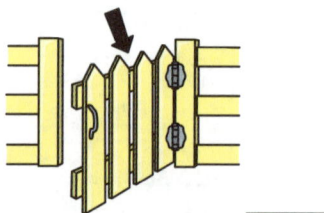
   ___

5.
   ___

6.
   ___

Addition/Place Value

Write each missing addend.

1. 9 + ☐ = 13
2. 6 + ☐ = 15
3. 9 + ☐ = 18
4. 4 + ☐ = 13
5. 4 + ☐ = 10
6. 7 + ☐ = 16
7. 7 + ☐ = 11
8. 6 + ☐ = 14
9. 8 + ☐ = 17
10. 8 + ☐ = 12
11. 5 + ☐ = 11
12. 12 + ☐ = 18

Count the tens and ones. Write each number.

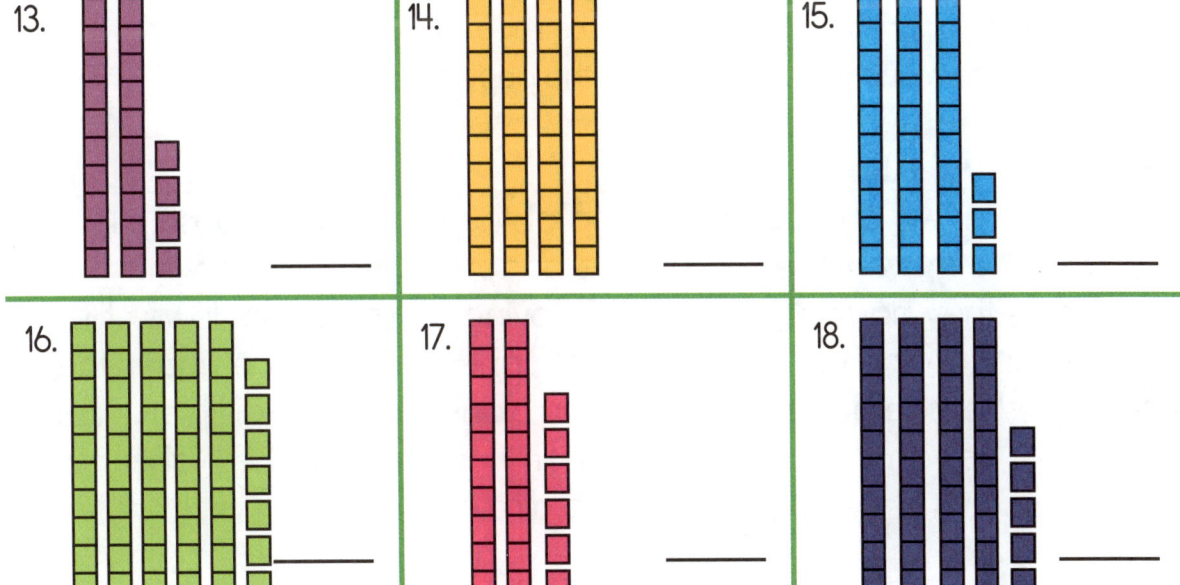

CHARACTER CHECK: Think of a family member who needs your help today. Help them accomplish a task, and you will both feel great.

DAY 7 — Science

The Flying Sheet of Paper

How do planes fly?

Materials:
- sheet of paper

Procedure:
1. Hold a sheet of paper just under your bottom lip. Curve the top of the paper slightly. What do you think will happen to the paper if you blow down and across the top of it? Do you think it will hit you in the chest, stay where it is, or bounce up and hit you in the nose?
2. Write your prediction on a separate sheet of paper.
3. Blow down and across the top of the paper.

What's This All About?
By blowing down and across the top of the paper, you cause air molecules to move faster across the paper rather than moving around as they normally do. Faster moving air molecules lower the air pressure on the top of the paper. Higher air pressure under the paper pushes the paper up. For an airplane to fly, the air pressure must be lower on top of the wings than under them. The higher air pressure under the wings pushes the airplane up.

More Fun Ideas to Try:
The next time you take a shower, notice what the shower curtain does. Does it balloon away, or does it move closer to you? Do you know why?

Language Arts & Grammar/Phonics   DAY 8

Rewrite each sentence below with a new verb. Look at the word in parentheses ( ) to see whether the new verb should be in the present, past, or future tense.

1. Sanja eats soup for lunch.

   (past) _____

2. Eli raced down the hill.

   (future) _____

3. Abby splashed her brother in the pool.

   (present) _____

4. The piano will need to be tuned.

   (present) _____

Say the name of each picture. Write the letter of each short vowel sound.

| 5.  ___ | 6.  ___ | 7.  ___ |
| 8. 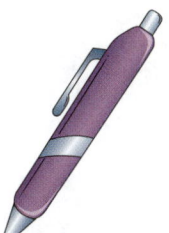 ___ | 9.  ___ | 10.  ___ |

13

DAY 9

Addition/Phonics

You can group addends in addition sentences in different ways without changing the sum. Write the missing numbers on the lines.

1. 4 + 8 + 2 = 4 + 10 = _____

2. 10 + _____ = 5 + 5 + 9 = 19

3. 6 + 6 + 4 = _____ + 6 = 16

4. 3 + 7 + _____ = 10 + 1 = 11

5. 9 + 1 + 8 = 10 + 8 = _____

6. 10 + 0 + 2 = 10 + _____ = 12

In a blend, like *sl* in *slide*, two consonants make a sound together. Say the name of each picture. Write the letters for the blend in each word.

7.
___ ___

8.
___ ___

9.
___ ___

10.
___ ___

11.
___ ___

12.
___ ___

Social Studies

International Cuisine

You can learn a lot about other countries by making and eating some of their native dishes. Think of a country you would like to know more about. Find out what foods the people from that country eat. For example, if you want to learn about France, go to the library with an adult and check out French cookbooks or books about French food. Or, search the Internet with an adult to find recipes for French dishes.

Choose a simple recipe with ingredients that you and an adult can buy at your local grocery store. Whether you make soup, salad, or another treat from the country, you will "taste" a bit of the country when you eat the food. Get your family involved. Invite each family member to choose a country and enjoy trying different foods from places around the world.

Take It Outside!

Outdoor Extension Activity

Grow a plant! All you need is a hand shovel, a seed or seedling, some soil, sunshine, and water. Ask an adult to help you choose what to plant and where to plant it. Whether you plant in a pot or in the ground, it's amazing to give new life to something special. After you plant the seed or seedling, put a paint stirrer or a wooden craft stick in the ground beside it. Then, use a pen to mark the plant's height as it grows taller. Spend the summer watering your plant and watching it grow! Draw pictures below of your plant as it grows. What does it look like at the beginning of summer, the middle of summer, and the end of summer?

beginning	middle	end

Outdoor Extension Activity

In many places, the weather is beautiful outside during the summer. The sun shines. Bright flowers bloom. Color is everywhere. Nature is as pretty as a picture. Make your own art from things that you find outside during the summer. Collect the objects that you discover, such as leaves, stones, shells, flowers, bark, and sticks. Then, make a colorful collage from your treasures. Draw a picture of your collage here.

DAY 11

Addition & Subtraction/Language Arts & Grammar

Look at each number in the apple. On the apple to the left, write the number that is 10 less than the number shown. On the apple to the right, write the number that is 10 more.

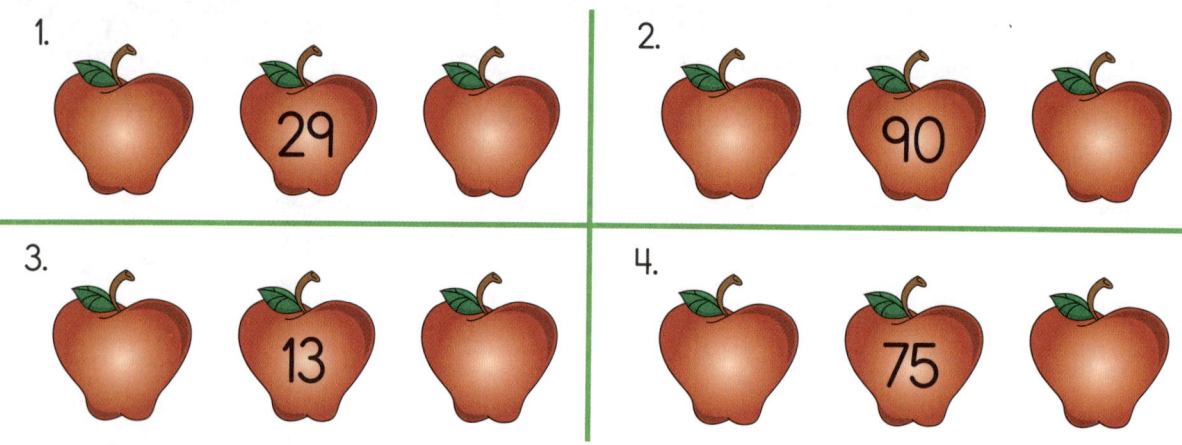

Unscramble each sentence. Write the words in the correct order.

5. swim like Ducks to.

   _____

6. we sandbox Can play in the?

   _____

7. nests birds in trees Some make.

   _____

8. fun today Are having you?

   _____

FITNESS FLASH: Do 10 shoulder shrugs.

* See page 2.

Addition & Subtraction/Language Arts & Grammar

DAY 12

Complete each fact family.

1. Family: 4, 9, 5

    4 + 5 = ☐

    5 + 4 = ☐

    9 − 5 = ☐

    9 − 4 = ☐

2. Family: 6, 2, 8

    6 + ☐ = 8

    2 + ☐ = ☐

    8 − ☐ = 2

    8 − ☐ = ☐

3. Family: 3, 7, 10

    ☐ + ☐ = ☐

    ☐ + ☐ = ☐

    ☐ − ☐ = ☐

    ☐ − ☐ = ☐

Read each noun in the box. Write it in the correct column.

Olivia	Dr. Yang	cousin
hippo	holiday	store
Greenlawn Library	Thanksgiving	

Common Nouns _____

Proper Nouns _____

19

© Carson Dellosa Education

DAY 13

Language Arts & Grammar

Write a letter to tell what kind of sentence each one is.

> S = Statement   Q = Question   C = Command   E = Exclamation

1. _____ What time does the game start?

2. _____ Zane just hit a home run!

3. _____ Pass me the bug spray.

4. _____ Oliver is on first base.

5. _____ Destiny is the fastest runner on our team.

Choose the conjunction that completes each sentence. Write it on the line.

6. Drew _____ Mom went to the farmers' market.
   (and, but)

7. Do you like corn _____ carrots better?
   (or, but)

8. The market had eggs, _____ we will have omelets today.
   (or, so)

9. Drew loves peas, _____ all the farmers were sold out.
   (but, because)

Language Arts & Grammar/Phonics

DAY 14

Rewrite each set of words below to make it show ownership.

EXAMPLE: the pear belonging to Peter

Peter's pear

1.

   the balloon belonging to Bella _____

2.

   the kite belonging to Kate _____

3.

   the hat belonging to Hasaan _____

4.

   the soccer ball belonging to Sammy _____

Say the name of each picture. Write **1** if the word has one syllable. Write **2** if the word has two syllables.

5.	6.	7.	8.

_____	_____	_____	_____

FACTOID: A sneeze can travel out of a person's mouth and nose at more than 100 miles (160 km) per hour.

DAY 15

Place Value/Writing

Write how many tens and ones are in each number.
EXAMPLE:

26 = __2__ tens __6__ ones

1. 41 = ____ tens ____ one
2. 45 = ____ tens ____ ones
3. 84 = ____ tens ____ ones
4. 65 = ____ tens ____ ones
5. 72 = ____ tens ____ ones
6. 17 = ____ tens ____ ones
7. 39 = ____ tens ____ ones
8. 50 = ____ tens ____ ones
9. 51 = ____ tens ____ one
10. 97 = ____ tens ____ ones
11. 100 = ____ tens ____ ones

Write a paragraph for a younger brother or sister, cousin, or friend. Explain how to do something step by step. You could explain how to feed a pet, make a sandwich, or plant a seed.

_____

_____

_____

_____

_____

_____

_____

Social Studies

My Own Map

Maps have many uses. A pilot uses maps to find the right flight paths. A hiker uses a map to find their way on a trail. A traveler uses a map to get around a new town.

Work on your mapmaking skills by drawing a map of a path that is in or around your home. You will need a sheet of paper and a pencil. Be as accurate as possible. If you are drawing a path from your room to the refrigerator, include hallways, stairways, rooms, and furniture that you pass as you walk.

Try your map when it is finished. Follow the path as you drew it. Make changes if needed. Then, have a friend or family member try your map. Ask them to use the map to follow the path to the end. Have a surprise treat waiting for them, such as a snack to share.

DAY 17

Number Relationships/Reading Comprehension

Write > or < to compare each set of numbers.

1. 11 ◯ 13   2. 91 ◯ 87   3. 55 ◯ 75

4. 46 ◯ 29   5. 39 ◯ 27   6. 78 ◯ 33

7. 24 ◯ 19   8. 73 ◯ 85   9. 48 ◯ 100

10. 14 ◯ 21   11. 62 ◯ 56   12. 94 ◯ 78

13. 18 ◯ 47   14. 54 ◯ 62   15. 50 ◯ 44

Number the sentences in the order that the events happened.

16. _____ The sun came out. It became a pretty day.

17. _____ It started to rain.

18. _____ Hannah put her umbrella away.

19. _____ Hannah used her umbrella.

20. _____ The clouds came, and the sky was dark.

FACTOID: Dust from Africa can travel all the way to Florida.

Time/Phonics

Write the correct time for each clock that has hands. Draw hands on each clock that has a time below it.

Say the name of each picture. Circle the letters that make each beginning sound.

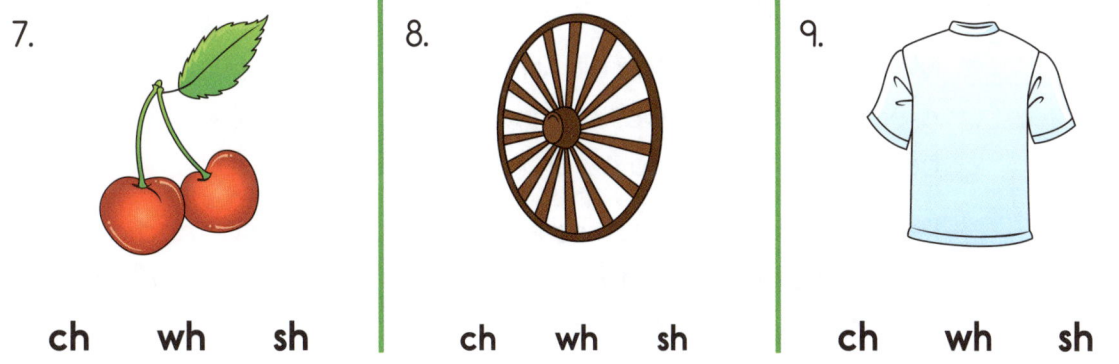

7. ch   wh   sh

8. ch   wh   sh

9. ch   wh   sh

DAY 19   **Measurement/Reading Comprehension**

Write 1, 2, or 3 on each line to order the objects from shortest to longest.

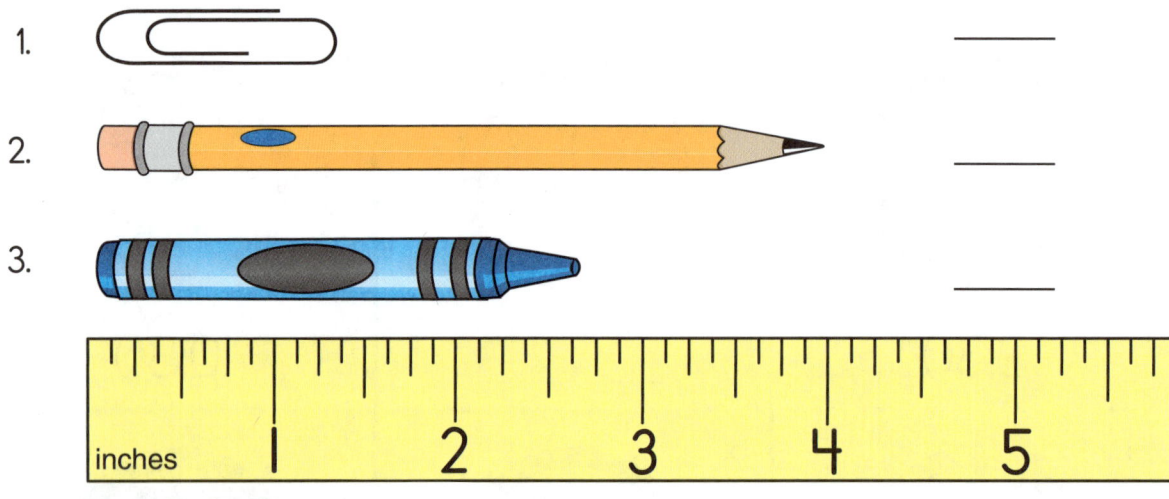

1. _____
2. _____
3. _____

A title tells what a story is about. Write the letter of the title next to the story it matches.

TITLES

A. The Turtle Dream   B. The Sleepover   C. A Wish Before Bed

4. _____ Jenna made a wish every night before going to sleep. She would look in the sky for the brightest star. Then, she would close her eyes and make a wish.

5. _____ Malia fell asleep in the car on the way to the beach. She dreamed that she was a flying turtle. She flew all around the beach. No one could catch her.

6. _____ Kendra had her friend Leslie sleep over. They watched a movie and ate popcorn. They made a tent out of blankets. They slept in the tent.

CHARACTER CHECK: Discuss with an adult what you think is the most important of all good manners.

Science

Upside-Down Water

Can you turn a cup of water upside down without spilling it?

Materials:
- index card
- clear plastic cup
- water

Procedure:
1. Do this experiment over a sink.
2. Fill the cup halfway with water.
3. Put the index card on top of the cup. Put your hand over the card. Turn the cup upside down over the sink.
4. Wait two seconds. Then, move your hand away.

What's This All About?
When you flip the cup, the air outside of the cup pushes on the card. The air pushes harder than the water inside the cup. If you wiggle the card before you move your hand, the water molecules on the card and the rim of the cup will stick together. Then, air cannot get in and equalize the pressure.

More Fun Ideas to Try:
- Use different amounts of water in the cup.
- Try different types of paper. You can use construction paper, wrapping paper or notebook paper.
- Find out how long you can hold the cup upside down before water starts to spill out.
- Try plastic cups of different sizes and shapes.
- Write a letter or an e-mail to a friend or relative. Tell about the experiment you did. Explain how it works and what your results were.

Take It Outside!

Outdoor Extension Activity

Head outside with a sheet of paper and pencil. Look around and list the things that you see, such as a bush, an ant, a cat, a sidewalk, a bee, a mailbox, a car, and a street. Sort the words into categories. Try to think of at least three ways to sort your words. For example, you could sort the words by their beginning sounds or by whether they name living or nonliving things.

Word List

Category: _____   Category: _____   Category: _____

Monthly Goals

Think of three goals that you would like to set for yourself this month. Have an adult help you write your goals on the lines. Place a sticker next to each of your goals that you complete.

1. _____ PLACE STICKER HERE

2. _____ PLACE STICKER HERE

3. _____ PLACE STICKER HERE

Introduction to Strength

This section includes fitness and character development activities that focus on strength. If your child has limited mobility, feel free to modify any suggested exercises to fit their individual abilities.

Physical Strength

Like flexibility, strength is an important component of good health. Explain that strength is built over time and point out to your child how much stronger they have become since they were a toddler.

Everyday activities and many fun exercises provide opportunities for children to gain strength. Your child could carry grocery bags to build their arms, ride a bicycle to develop their legs, or swim for a full-body strength workout. Help your child set realistic, achievable goals to improve their strength based on the activities that they enjoy.

Strength of Character

Guide your child to work on inner strength as well. Explain that having strong character means respectfully standing up for their values, even if others do not agree with their viewpoint.

Discuss real-life examples, such as a time that they may have been teased by another child. How did they use inner strength to handle the situation? Explain to your child they can show strength by being honest, by standing up for someone who needs help, and by putting their best efforts into every task. Remember to acknowledge moments your child has demonstrated strength of character so they can see the positive growth.

DAY 1 Counting/Language Arts & Grammar

Skip-count by fives. Fill in the missing numbers.

1.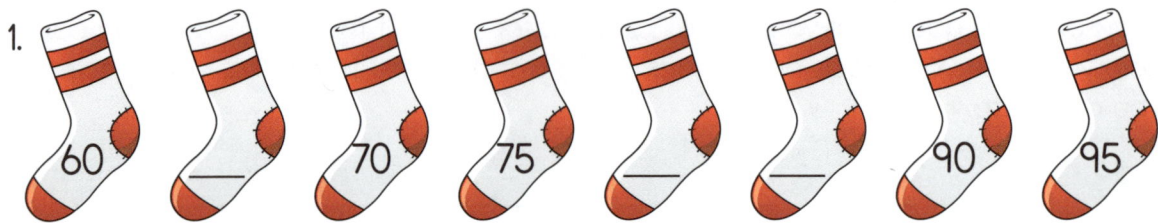
60, ___, 70, 75, ___, ___, 90, 95

Skip-count by tens. Fill in the missing numbers.

2.
320, ___, 340, 350, ___, 370, ___, 390

Skip-count by hundreds. Fill in the missing numbers.

3.
300, 400, ___, ___, 700, ___, 900, 1,000

Write adjectives to describe each object.

4. teddy bear

5. gift

Addition/Phonics

DAY 2

Follow the directions to solve each problem.

1. Start with 54. Write the number that is 100 more. _____

2. Start with 80. Write the number that is 10 more. _____

3. Start with 22. Write the number that is 100 more. _____

4. Start with 65. Write the number that is 10 more. _____

Circle the word that names each picture. Write the word on the line.

5.  glove

glue

6.  frog

flag

7.  clown

clock

8.  bow

bowl

FACTOID: Sloths move so slowly that green algae can grow on their fur.

DAY 3  Reading Comprehension/Language Arts & Grammar

Read each paragraph. Circle the letter of the best title.

1. Carlos is at bat. He hits the ball. He runs to first base and then to second base. Will Carlos make it all of the way to home plate?

    A. Running
    B. Carlos Likes to Play
    C. Carlos's Baseball Game

2. Madison put on sunscreen and sunglasses. Then, she found her favorite green hat. Madison was ready to go outside.

    A. A Rainy Day
    B. Ready to Go Out in the Sun
    C. Madison Likes to Play

Draw a line to match each contraction to its word pair.

EXAMPLE:

didn't ——————————————————— it is

3. it's   we will
4. we're ——————————————————— did not
5. you've   we are
6. don't   is not
7. we'll   you have
8. isn't   do not

FITNESS FLASH: Do 10 lunges.

* See page 2.

Social Studies

Look What I Did!

A time line is a list of dates that tells important things that have happened. You have already had a lot of things happen in your lifetime. Make a time line to show your accomplishments, milestones, and important events. Ask an adult to help you. If you have a baby book, scrapbooks, photo albums, or other records, use those things to help, too. You will need a piece of poster board and markers to create the time line. List at least 10 different events to show a variety of activities. If possible, attach photos or drawings to highlight the events. This is a fun way to look back at your history. Display the time line in a special place in your bedroom. Add to it as you grow and do more.

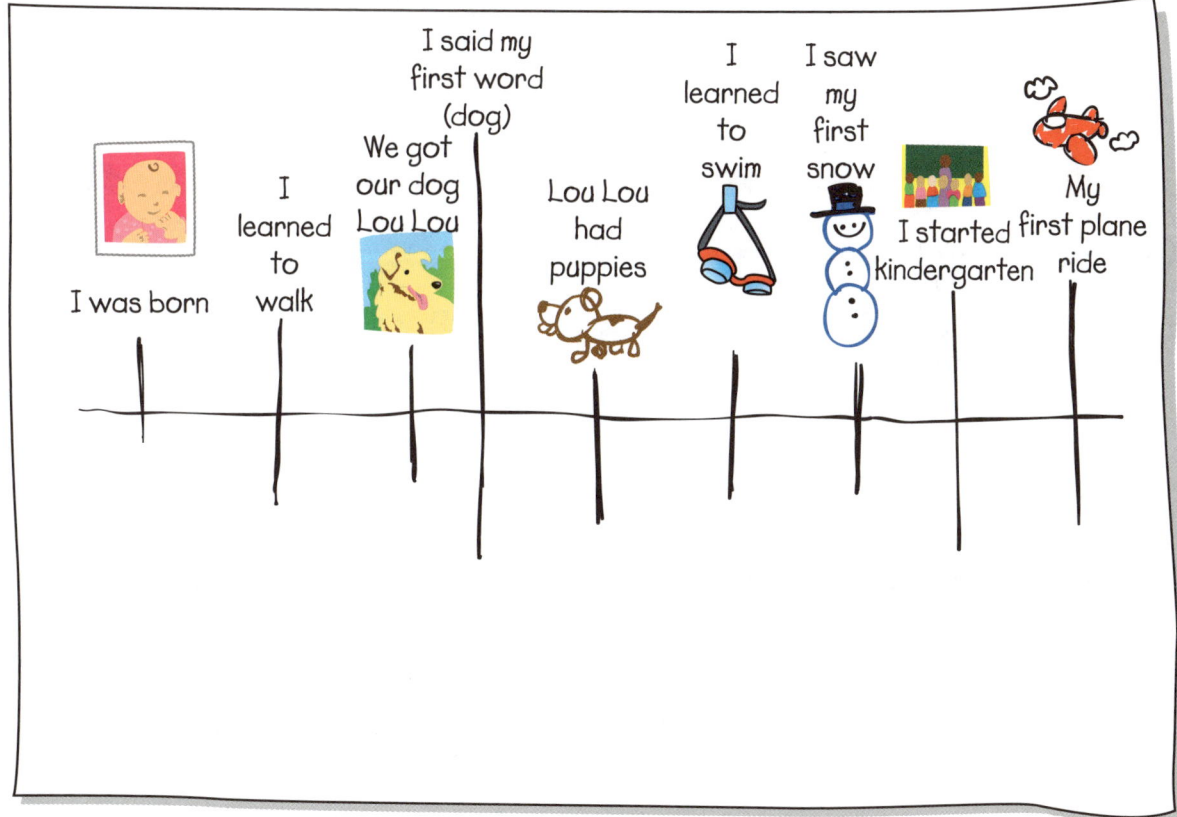

DAY 5

Problem Solving/Addition & Subtraction

1. Lori bought an umbrella and a book. How much money did she spend?

2. Henry bought a yo-yo and an umbrella. How much money did he spend?

3. Maria bought a baseball and a yo-yo. How much money did she spend?

4. Alejandro bought a baseball and a book. How much money did he spend?

Add to find each sum.

5. 5
  +7

6. 8
  +4

7. 3
  +7

8. 9
  +5

9. 15
  + 2

10. 10
  + 6

Subtract to find each difference.

11. 12
  − 8

12. 9
  −4

13. 11
  − 7

14. 8
  −8

15. 10
  − 2

16. 16
  − 2

Language Arts & Grammar/Numbers

Similar words can have different shades of meaning. Underline the word that best completes each sentence.

1. Jamilla carefully (sipped, gulped) the hot tea.
2. Dana (tapped, pounded) on her parents' door when she heard the fire alarm.
3. Lex felt (nervous, terrified) when he realized he had forgotten his permission slip.
4. Dad was (tired, exhausted) after driving all through the night to get home.

How many are in each group? Write the number on the line. Then, circle *odd* or *even*.

5.

   _____ odd   even

6.

   _____ odd   even

7.

   _____ odd   even

8. 🐐🐐 🐐🐐 🐐

   _____ odd   even

DAY 7 Phonics/Spelling

Say each word in the box. Listen for the long vowel sound. Write the word under the correct heading.

bugle	apron	bedtime	Monday	human
eagle	rider	argue	flavor	hello
frozen	ocean	unkind	season	fever

Long a   Long e   Long i   Long o   Long u

_____ _____ _____ _____ _____

_____ _____ _____ _____ _____

_____ _____ _____ _____ _____

Underline the misspelled word in each sentence. Then, write each misspelled word correctly on the line.

1. What may I help yu with? _____

2. Please giv him a fork. _____

3. You can sti on the chair. _____

4. Will you miks the paint? _____

FITNESS FLASH: Do five push-ups.

* See page 2.

Science

DAY 8

Super Sediment

What sinks to the bottom of a river first: soil, sand, or pebbles?

Materials:
- 3 paper cups
- funnel
- pebbles
- soda bottle (2-liter with cap)
- sand
- soil
- water

Procedure:

1. Fill one paper cup with soil, one cup with sand, and one cup with pebbles. These will be the sediment.
2. Use the funnel to pour the soil, sand, and pebbles into the bottle. Pour water into the bottle until it is almost full. Close the cap tightly.
3. Shake the bottle until everything is mixed well.
4. Place the bottle on a table. On a separate sheet of paper, draw a picture of what you see in the bottle. Watch as the sediment begins to settle in the bottle.
5. Check the bottle after 15–30 minutes. Draw what you see.
6. Check the bottle again in 24 hours. Draw what you see.

What's This All About?

Sediment is the soil, sand, and pebbles that wash into streams, rivers, and lakes. In nature, sediment piles up and forms sedimentary rocks.

In the bottle, you have created a small body of water with a lot of sediment. The larger pieces of sediment settle to the bottom more quickly. The smaller pieces of sediment are more likely to float in the water longer and settle to the bottom more slowly.

Think About It

- What is a funnel? Why do you need to use one to get the materials into the bottle?
- Which section of the experiment tells you what to do, step by step?

* See page 2.

DAY 9 Graphing

Which flavor of ice-cream is the most popular with your friends and family? Ask each person to choose a favorite ice-cream flavor from the list. Make a tally mark beside each answer given.

vanilla _____   banana _____

chocolate _____   cherry _____

strawberry _____   other _____

Count the tally marks beside each flavor. Graph your results.

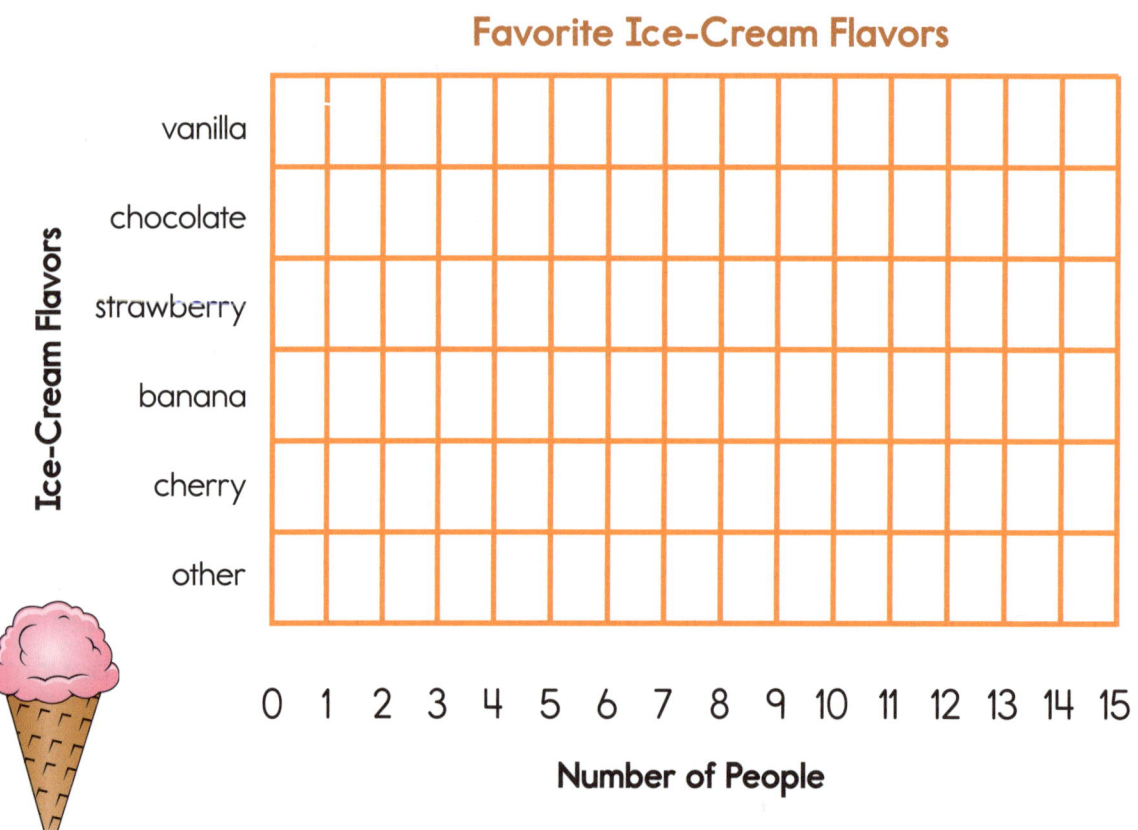

CHARACTER CHECK: Form a neighborhood cleanup crew. With an adult and some friends, walk through your neighborhood and pick up litter. Your neighborhood will be a cleaner place!

Subtraction/Spelling

DAY 10

Draw a line to match each pair that has the same difference.

1.	5 – 3	5 – 1		2.	8 – 7	10 – 4
	8 – 3	9 – 8			3 – 1	4 – 3
	8 – 4	7 – 2			8 – 2	5 – 3
	5 – 4	6 – 4			9 – 5	7 – 3
3.	10 – 5	13 – 10		4.	5 – 5	14 – 7
	12 – 6	7 – 1			12 – 9	8 – 5
	2 – 0	9 – 4			11 – 4	8 – 8
	9 – 6	4 – 2			12 – 8	5 – 1

Unscramble each word. Spell each word correctly on the line to complete each sentence.

5. Juan had a _____ for _____ mother.
                     igft   **ihs**

6. The _____ has a _____ tire.
         acr   **tfla**

7. A butterfly _____ on _____ flower.
              ats   **hte**

8. My _____ works at the _____.
         add   **tsoer**

> **FACTOID:** You'll never see elephants playing hopscotch. Why? Because they can't jump!

Take It Outside!

Outdoor Extension Activity

Set up a safe, mini-obstacle course in a grassy area. Use soft objects, such as piles of cut grass or piles of leaves. Arrange the items in a line. When you reach the end of the course, turn around and retrace your steps to repeat it. Vary the way that you go through the course, such as running, hopping, crabwalking, or skipping. Then, write five sentences about your mini-obstacle course. What objects did you use? What part did you like best? What would you add next time?

_____

_____

_____

_____

_____

_____

_____

_____

_____

_____

Outdoor Extension Activity

Take a friend, sibling, or parent outside with you and challenge them to a "rhyme-off." Find a spot to sit down and begin by pointing out an object that you see, such as a rose. Invite your partner to think of a real word that rhymes with *rose*, such as *nose*. (*Zose* will not work.) Go back and forth until neither of you can think of any other rhyming words. Then, pick a new outside word and start again. Draw a picture of the objects you find and write the rhyming words on the lines beside.

_____

_____

_____

_____

_____

_____

_____

_____

_____

DAY 11  Phonics/Spelling

Read each word. Write *e* if the *y* makes the long *e* sound, as in *story*. Write *i* if the *y* makes the long *i* sound, as in *sky*.

1. ☐ baby ☐ fly ☐ windy ☐ bunny ☐ fry

2. ☐ shy ☐ family ☐ buy ☐ happy ☐ jelly

3. ☐ cry ☐ my ☐ funny ☐ silly ☐ try

Write words to fill the blanks.

Singular (One)	Plural (More Than One)
child	_____
mouse	_____
_____	feet
man	_____
_____	teeth
_____	people

FITNESS FLASH: Do 10 squats.

* See page 2.

Addition/Counting

DAY 12

Add to find each sum. Draw a line to match each dog with the correct bone.

1. 32
   +21

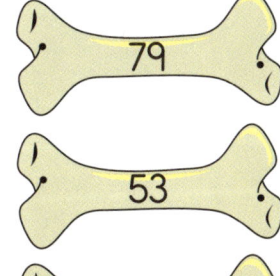

4. 44
   +13

2. 73
   +24

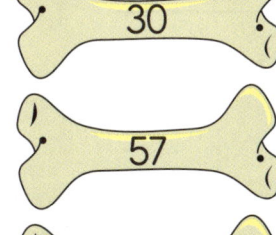

5. 52
   +26

3. 20
   +10

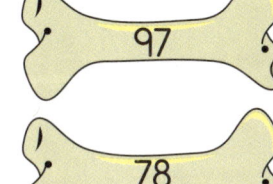

6. 61
   +18

Complete each number line.

Count by twos.

7.

   2   4   6   ___   ___   ___

Count by fives.

8.

   5   ___   15   ___   ___   30

CHARACTER CHECK: Talk with an adult about the best time and way to ask for something.

DAY 13 Geometry/Language Arts & Grammar

Draw lines to divide each rectangle into rows and columns. Then, count how many squares there are. Write your answer on the line.

1. 3 rows
   4 columns

   How many squares? _____

2. 4 rows
   5 columns

   How many squares? _____

Read each sentence and circle each noun. A noun can be a person, place, or thing.

3. The boy lost his shoe.

4. She wrote a letter to her aunt.

5. Did you have a sandwich?

6. We saw a movie about butterflies.

7. My little sister has a shiny ring.

FACTOID: Some types of bamboo can grow more than 40 in. (100 cm) per day.

Language Arts & Grammar/Reading Comprehension **DAY 14**

Draw a line to divide each compound word into two words. Write the words on the line.

1. goldfish
   _____

2. popcorn
   _____

3. daytime
   _____

4. doghouse
   _____

5. spaceship
   _____

6. railroad
   _____

7. blueberry
   _____

8. sailboat
   _____

9. grapefruit
   _____

10. cupcake
    _____

11. newspaper
    _____

12. sometime
    _____

Number the sentences in the order that the events happened.

13. _____ Jenny made a chocolate cake for her friend.

14. _____ Jenny put blue frosting on the cake.

15. _____ Jenny put sprinkles on the cake.

16. _____ Jenny went to the store and bought a box of cake mix.

DAY 15

Addition & Subtraction/Language Arts & Grammar

Write the correct numbers to get the answer in each box.

1. 4 − _____ =
   3 + _____ = **3**
   2 + _____ =

2. 5 + _____ =
   2 + _____ = **6**
   9 − _____ =

3. 7 + _____ =
   _____ − 1 = **8**
   _____ − 3 =

4. _____ − 4 =
   8 − _____ = **5**
   3 + _____ =

Write the correct contractions.

5. cannot _____
6. I am _____
7. you are _____
8. do not _____
9. he is _____
10. I will _____

Write the two words in each contraction.

11. didn't _____
12. isn't _____
13. you've _____
14. she's _____
15. couldn't _____
16. we're _____

CHARACTER CHECK: Discuss with an adult what you think are the three most important qualities of a good friend.

46

Language Arts & Grammar

DAY 16

Write *is* or *are* to complete each sentence.

1. We _____ going to town tomorrow.

2. This book _____ not mine.

3. Where _____ a box of cereal?

4. Seals _____ fast swimmers.

5. _____ he planning to help?

6. _____ you going to the festival?

Write a sentence using *is*.

_____

Write a sentence using *are*.

_____

Write the correct punctuation mark at the end of each sentence. Use the marks (.), (!), or (?).

7. Are we going to the park _____

8. Look out for the ball _____

9. I know you can do it _____

10. Do bulls have horns on their heads _____

11. The girl on the bike is my sister _____

DAY 17

Social Studies

Having a Ball on Earth

A globe is a 3-D map that shows what Earth looks like. Make your own globe with a beach ball or large plastic ball and markers. Draw a line around the middle of the ball to represent the equator. The equator is a pretend line that marks the middle of the world. Label the top of the ball *north pole* and the bottom of the ball *south pole*. The north and south poles are places that mark the top and the bottom of Earth. Draw and label the seven continents (Africa, Antarctica, Asia, Australia, Europe, North America, and South America) and the five major oceans (Arctic, Atlantic, Indian, Pacific, and Southern). Place a star sticker on the globe to represent the place where you live. Toss the globe around with a friend or family member, and try to learn the names of the important places that you marked. Soon, you will know more about Earth than you did before.

Language Arts & Grammar

DAY 18

Holidays and product names begin with a capital letter. Underline each letter that should be a capital three times (b̲).

1. On valentine's day, Dad cooked a fancy dinner for Mom.

2. At the grocery store, we bought two boxes of tasty crunch granola bars.

3. We'll be back from vacation on labor day.

4. Scout and Otis are almost out of chicken nibblers dog treats.

Pronouns take the place of nouns. A *reflexive pronoun* is a special type of pronoun that ends in *–self* or *–selves*. Circle the reflexive pronoun in each sentence.

5. Rico and I gave ourselves half an hour to get ready.

6. The girls were proud of themselves for winning the game.

7. You know yourself better than anyone else does.

8. Josie tried to give herself a haircut when she was two!

9. I told myself not to be scared as I entered the dark room.

FITNESS FLASH: Do five push-ups.

* See page 2.

49

DAY 19

Science

Sweet, Sour, Salty, Bitter

Did you know that you can make a taste map of your tongue?

Materials:
- lemon (cut in half)
- pretzel
- water
- grapefruit rind
- sugar cube

Procedure:
1. Touch the inside of a lemon to the very tip of your tongue. Do you taste it? Don't move your tongue around. Rinse your mouth with water. Touch the lemon to the middle of your tongue. Do you taste it? Rinse your mouth with water. Touch the lemon to the sides of your tongue. Do you taste it?
2. Rinse your mouth with water. Repeat the activity with the pretzel, the grapefruit, and finally the sugar cube.

What's This All About?
There are four main tastes that humans can tell apart: sweet, sour, salty, and bitter. Your tongue is divided into different taste zones. Each taste zone is a certain area of your tongue. In this activity, you should discover which parts of your tongue detect each kind of taste.

More Fun Ideas to Try:
Based on your experiment, draw a taste map of your tongue. First, draw a picture of your tongue in the box. Then, label each area where you tasted salty, sweet, sour, and bitter.

* See page 2.

Money/Language Arts & Grammar

DAY 20

Circle the coins that add up to the amount shown.

1.

   10¢

2.

   16¢

3.

   25¢

4.

   45¢

Write the meaning of each word. Use the meanings of the prefixes to help you.

> un– = not   dis– = not, opposite of
> re– = again   pre– = before

5. unsafe = _____

6. rebuild = _____

7. dislike = _____

8. precook = _____

Take It Outside!

Outdoor Extension Activity

Play outdoor opposites. The park is perfect for this game. While you're there, look around. Try to find opposite events that are happening. For example, you might see a sad toddler who fell when playing and a happy dog rolling in the grass. See how many opposites you can find! Draw a picture in each box of the opposites you found.

Monthly Goals

Think of three goals that you would like to set for yourself this month. Have an adult help you write your goals on the lines. Place a sticker next to each of your goals that you complete.

1. _____ [PLACE STICKER HERE]

2. _____ [PLACE STICKER HERE]

3. _____ [PLACE STICKER HERE]

Introduction to Endurance

This section includes fitness and character development activities that focus on endurance. If your child has limited mobility, feel free to modify any suggested exercises to fit their individual abilities.

Physical Endurance

Improving endurance requires regular aerobic exercise, which causes the heart to beat faster and the person to breathe harder. There are many ways for a child to get an aerobic workout that does not feel like exercise. Jumping rope and playing tag are examples.

If you see your child head for a screen, suggest an activity that will get them moving instead. Explain that a relaxing indoor activity can be valuable, but it is important to take advantage of the warm and sunny days to go outdoors. Reserve the less active times for when it is dark, too hot, or raining. Explain the importance of physical activity and invite them to join you for a walk or a bike ride.

Endurance and Character Development

Explain to your child that mental endurance means to stick with something. For example, staying with a task when they might want to quit and keeping at it until it is done are ways that a child can show endurance.

Look for situations where your child might seem frustrated or bored. Explain that quitting should be the last resort. Teaching your child at a young age to endure will help them as they continue to develop into a happy, healthy person.

DAY 1   **Language Arts & Grammar/Spelling**

Combine each pair of sentences into a compound sentence. Use the conjunction in parentheses ( ). Make sure to put a comma before each conjunction.

EXAMPLE: Malik mowed the yard. He didn't weed the garden. (but)
Malik mowed the yard, but he didn't weed the garden.

1. Jackson made a fruit salad. Lena brought dessert. (and)
   _____

2. The bunny hopped across the yard. The cat did not see it. (but)
   _____

3. I could hear the rain on the roof. I knew the storm had begun. (so)
   _____

4. Julia walks to school with Chase. She rides the bus. (or)
   _____

Circle the word that is spelled correctly in each row.

5.	ca'nt	can'nt	can't
6.	esy	easy	eazy
7.	kea	key	kee
8.	buy	buye	biy
9.	liht	light	ligte
10.	wonce	onse	once
11.	carry	carey	carre
12.	you're	yure	yo're
13.	star	stor	starr
14.	funy	funny	funnie

54

Measurement/Spelling

DAY 2

Use the mileage maps to answer the questions.

1. How many miles is it from Salt Lake City to Bountiful? _____

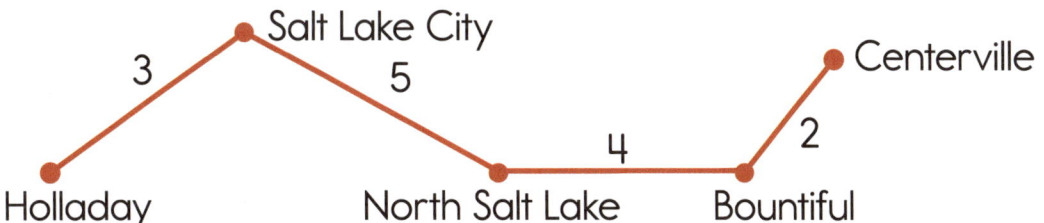

2. How many miles is it from Provo to Pleasant Grove? _____

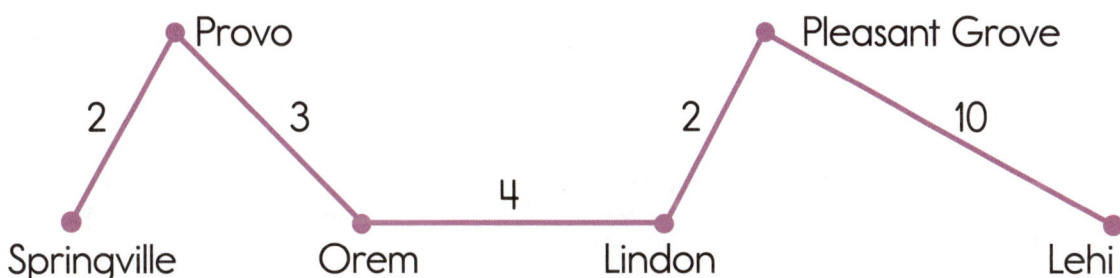

Read each sentence. If the underlined word is spelled correctly, circle *yes*. If the underlined word is not spelled correctly, circle *no*.

3.	Uma is a very <u>brav</u> girl.	yes	no
4.	The United States flag is red, white, and <u>bloo</u>.	yes	no
5.	Those girls were in my <u>class</u>.	yes	no
6.	Gina is a very <u>helpfull</u> friend.	yes	no
7.	I turned off the <u>light</u>.	yes	no
8.	This glue is sticky <u>stuf</u>.	yes	no
9.	Is <u>shee</u> coming with us?	yes	no

FITNESS FLASH: Do 10 jumping jacks.

* See page 2.

DAY 3 Addition & Subtraction/Measurement

Add or subtract to solve each problem.

1. 29
  +12

2. 28
  +43

3. 67
  +26

4. 42
  +39

5. 89
  +11

6. 76
  +24

7. 67
  −40

8. 83
  −20

9. 77
  −10

10. 76
  −50

11. 59
  −30

12. 77
  −60

Measure each item in centimeters. Then, answer the questions.

13.

How long is the alligator? _____

How long is the saw? _____

How much longer is the alligator than the saw? _____

14.

How long is the guitar? _____

How long is the violin? _____

How much longer is the guitar than the violin? _____

Numbers/Problem Solving **DAY 4**

Write the numeral for each number word.

1. nine hundred ninety-six ____
2. twenty-one ____
3. eighty-two ____
4. thirty-seven ____
5. two hundred sixty-five ____
6. six hundred sixty-one ____
7. seventy-nine ____
8. fifty-eight ____
9. twenty-two ____
10. seven hundred eighty ____
11. one hundred eighteen ____
12. one hundred ____

Solve each problem. Write your answer on the line.

13. Silas is 54 inches tall. Lily is 8 inches shorter than he is. How tall is Lily?

    _____

14. Anton picked 18 sunflowers, Luis picked 14, and Lola picked 26. How many sunflowers did they pick in all? _____

15. Noah and Aylen are collecting canned food for a food drive. On Monday, they collected 56 cans. On Tuesday, they collected 36 cans. How many cans did they collect in all? _____

16. Kris saved up $45. He decided to buy a skateboard for $27. How much money did he have left? _____

DAY 5

Problem Solving/Reading Comprehension

Solve each problem.

1. There are 26 students on one bus. There are 29 students on the other bus. How many students are on the buses altogether?

2. Nia found 47 shells on the beach. Byron found 44 shells on the beach. How many shells did they find in all?

3. Kamal ran 15 laps on Monday. He ran 17 laps on Tuesday. How many laps did Kamal run altogether?

4. Thomas saw 48 fish in one fish tank. Brooke saw 36 fish in another fish tank. How many fish did they see in all?

Read the story. Circle each answer that makes sense. There may be more than one answer.

5. Murphy's mom quickly pulled everything out of the dryer. Then, she lifted the lid of the washer, looked inside, and shook her head. She looked around the kitchen and family room, and then she rushed upstairs. "I cannot find it," she called to Murphy. "The last time I saw it was after the game on Saturday. We have to find it before 4:00!"

   A. Murphy's mom has friends coming over at 4:00.

   B. Murphy's mom is looking for Murphy's soccer jersey.

   C. Murphy has a game today at 4:00.

   D. Murphy's mom lost her purse.

Science  DAY 6

Catching Ice Cubes

Can you use salt and a piece of string to "catch" an ice cube?

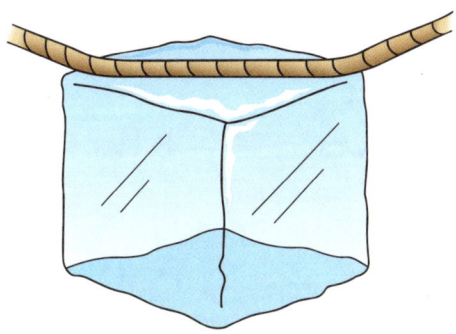

Materials:
- ice cube
- salt
- string

Procedure:
1. Try to catch the ice cube with the piece of string. (You cannot tie the string around the ice cube.) Can you do it?
2. Next, place the string on the ice cube and sprinkle a little salt on the string. Count to 30 and slowly lift the string. The ice cube will be attached!

What's This All About?
When you sprinkle salt on the ice, it lowers the freezing temperature of the ice. This causes some water to melt around the string. When the water forms, it **dilutes** the salt on the ice and allows the water to freeze around the string. This is why you can pick it up.

Think About It
- Why do you have to count to 30 before you lift the string?
- In the last paragraph, what do you think *dilutes* means?

 **FITNESS FLASH:** Hop on your right foot for 30 seconds.

* See page 2.

DAY 7

Reading Comprehension/Writing

Write the letter of each cause beside its effect.

Effects   Causes

1. _____ Justin put on his mittens.   A. It was cold outside.

2. _____ Chloe put ice in the water.   B. Her feet had grown.

3. _____ Ahmet gave his dog a bath.   C. The bike's tires were flat.

4. _____ Evan put air in his bike tires.   D. The rabbit was hungry.

5. _____ Kari got a new pair of shoes.   E. The water was warm.

6. _____ The rabbit ate the carrot.   F. The dog played in the mud.

Imagine that you are going on a trip. You can take only one thing. What would you take? Why?

_____

_____

_____

_____

CHARACTER CHECK: Make a list of things you can do to show respect to animals.

Social Studies

Animals Around the World

Studying animals is a great way to learn about different places in the world. Go to the library and check out books about animals that live in other parts of the world. You can also search the Internet with an adult to find out about animals. Choose an animal that lives on each continent (Africa, Antarctica, Asia, Australia, Europe, North America, and South America). As you read about each animal, you may find that the climate (weather patterns) or the food that grows in a place affects which animals live there. On the chart, write the name of each animal, the continent on which it lives, and why it lives there.

ANIMAL	CONTINENT	WHY IT LIVES THERE

DAY 9

Problem Solving/Reading Comprehension

Use the chart to answer each question.

Allowance for Each Chore Completed

Bundle newspapers for recycling	$0.25
Empty wastepaper baskets	$0.75
Put away groceries	$0.50
Wash the car	$2.00
Set the table	$1.00

1. Which chore pays the most money? _____

2. If Hugo sets the table for dinner every night this week, how much will he earn? _____

3. Davis bundled newspapers for recycling two times this week. How much money did he earn? _____

Read each statement. Write *Y* for *yes* or *N* for *no* beside each statement.

How a Snake Is Like a Turtle

4. _____ Both have shells.

5. _____ Both can be on land.

6. _____ Both are reptiles.

7. _____ Both have scales.

How a Bike Is Like a Truck

8. _____ Both have tires.

9. _____ Both need gas.

10. _____ Both can be new.

11. _____ Both have four wheels.

FACTOID: Yo-yos have ridden on at least two NASA spacecraft.

Geometry/Graphing

DAY 10

Follow the directions to color the shapes.

1.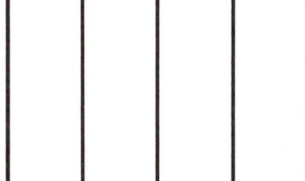

   Color three fourths.

2.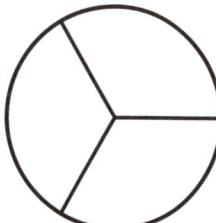

   Color one third.

3.

   Color one fourth.

4.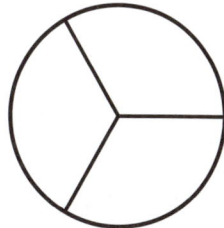

   Color two thirds.

The bar graph shows concession stand sales at a baseball game. Use the bar graph to answer the questions.

5. Do people buy more nachos or fruit bowls?

   _____

6. How many more fruit bowls than pretzels were sold? _____

7. People bought more than 50 of which item?

   _____

Take It Outside!

Outdoor Extension Activity

Collect several different small outdoor objects: a pinecone, a leaf, a flower, a nut, a rock, and other safe, interesting outdoor things. Put each item on the ground. Look at it. Decide whether each item is symmetrical. *Symmetrical* means that if you cut something in half, the two sides will look the same and have the same parts. If they do, then the object is symmetrical. If they do not, then the object is asymmetrical. Draw the objects you found in the boxes below. If the object is symmetrical, draw a line down the middle to show the two identical sides.

Symmetrical	Asymmetrical

Outdoor Extension Activity

Go for a walk! As you go, write 6 things you see. Then, write two words to describe each thing. This is good practice for writing adjectives and a great way to take a look at nature.

ADJECTIVES

1. _____   _____
                              _____

2. _____   _____
                              _____

3. _____   _____
                              _____

4. _____   _____
                              _____

5. _____   _____
                              _____

6. _____   _____
                              _____

DAY 11

Problem Solving/Phonics

Solve each problem.

> **EXAMPLE:**
> Nick left for school on the bus at 8:00. The bus ride took 20 minutes. What time did Nick get to school?
> Think: 8:00 + 0:20 = 8:20

1. Claire ate a snack at 10:00. She ate lunch 2 hours later. What time did she eat lunch?

   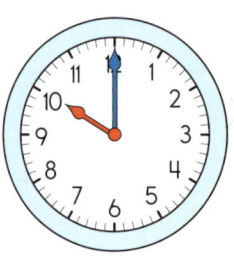

   _____

2. This morning, Hau read for 15 minutes. He started at 9:00. What time did he finish reading?

   _____

3. Recess lasted 30 minutes. It started at 2:00. What time did it end?

   _____

4. Ellis left school at 3:30. He rode the bus for 30 minutes. What time did he get off of the bus?

   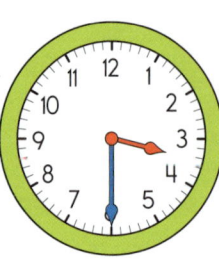

   _____

Say each word aloud. Write the syllables in the boxes.

5. apartment

6. enormous

7. subtraction

8. wonderful

Patterning/Vocabulary

DAY 12

Complete each number pattern. Write the rule.

1. 2, 4, 6, 8, _____ , _____ , _____ , _____ , _____ , _____

   Rule: _____

2. 5, 10, 15, _____ , _____ , _____ , _____ , _____ , _____

   Rule: _____

3. 3, 6, 9, 12, _____ , _____ , _____ , _____ , _____ , _____

   Rule: _____

Use the words from the word bank to complete each analogy. An *analogy* is a way to show how things are alike. To complete an analogy, look at the first set of words. Decide how they are related. Apply that relationship to the second set of words.

EXAMPLE: *Finger : hand :: toe : _____.* (A *finger* is part of a *hand*. What is a *toe* a part of? The answer is *foot*.)

| light | sky | square | table |

4. sleep : bed :: eat : _____

5. three : triangle :: four : _____

6. green : grass :: blue : _____

7. win : lose :: dark : _____

FACTOID: Dragonflies can fly at speeds of up to 40 mph (64 km/h).

Addition/Reading Comprehension

Repeated addition problems help you get ready for multiplication. Add to find each sum.

1. 3
    3
    + 3
    ___

2. 2
    2
    + 2
    ___

3. 4
    4
    + 4
    ___

4. 5
    5
    + 5
    ___

5. 3
    3
    3
    + 3
    ___

6. 2
    2
    2
    + 2
    ___

7. 5
    5
    5
    + 5
    ___

8. 4
    4
    4
    + 4
    ___

A *glossary* is found at the back of a book. It tells what certain words in the book mean. Use this glossary from a book about deserts to answer the questions below.

> **arid** something that is very dry
> **camouflage** coloring that helps an animal hide
> **desert** an environment where very little rain falls; home to few plants and animals
> **evaporate** to change from a liquid into a gas
> **precipitation** any kind of water that falls from the sky (like rain, snow, hail, etc.)

9. What does *evaporate* mean? _____

10. A moth that blends in with the bark on a tree is using _____ .

11. If a place is arid, it is very _____ .

12. What is one example of precipitation? _____

Social Studies

Earth Effects

Earth is a big place. Did you know that what you do every day can affect the planet? Almost every human action does something to Earth. Think about this: If a family goes to the beach for the day and leaves behind a few soft drink cans, a newspaper, and an empty sunscreen bottle, they have had a negative effect on our planet. But, if they had simply taken the items with them and dropped them off in recycling bins, they would have had a positive effect on Earth. The metal cans, newspaper, and sunscreen bottle could be recycled and made into something new. Trash would not have littered the beach. The ocean animals would not have been hurt by the trash left behind.

Do you want to have a positive effect on Earth? Have your family members help you make a list of things you can do to be good to the planet.

_____

_____

_____

_____

_____

_____

_____

_____

DAY 15

Place Value/Addition & Subtraction

Write the expanded form for each number.
EXAMPLE:

251 = __2__ hundreds + __5__ tens + __1__ one = __200__ + __50__ + __1__

1. 341 = _____ hundreds + _____ tens + _____ one = _____ + _____ + _____

2. 563 = _____ hundreds + _____ tens + _____ ones = _____ + _____ + _____

3. 752 = _____ hundreds + _____ tens + _____ ones = _____ + _____ + _____

4. 845 = _____ hundreds + _____ tens + _____ ones = _____ + _____ + _____

Use the number line to help you solve each problem. Mark the number line to show your work.

5. 25 + 40 = _____

6. 56 + 18 = _____

7. 90 − 60 = _____

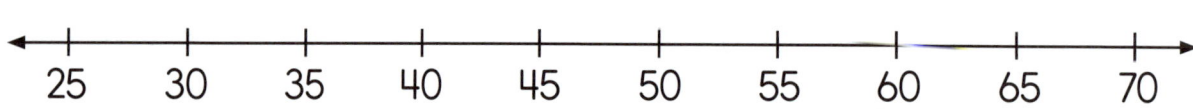

CHARACTER CHECK: Discuss with an adult why it is sometimes difficult to break bad habits.

Number Relationships/Reading Comprehension **DAY 16**

Write > (greater than) or < (less than) to compare each pair of numbers.

1. 103 ◯ 111
2. 640 ◯ 460
3. 322 ◯ 100
4. 190 ◯ 910
5. 290 ◯ 300
6. 985 ◯ 850
7. 140 ◯ 400
8. 124 ◯ 216
9. 648 ◯ 846
10. 680 ◯ 480
11. 592 ◯ 324
12. 745 ◯ 746

Read the story.

Winter Fun

Some people like spring, but I do not. I think that winter is the best season. My family goes to the mountains every year. My stepmom is a good skier. She skis while we watch. My dad wears snowshoes and goes on long walks. My brothers and I like to play in the snow. The nights are too cold to be outside. So, we stay warm in our cabin. My stepmom makes us hot chocolate at bedtime, and we tell stories.

Decide whether each sentence is a fact or an opinion. Write F for fact or O for opinion.

13. _____ Winter is the best season.
14. _____ My family goes to the mountains.
15. _____ My stepmom makes us hot chocolate.
16. _____ I think my stepmom is a good skier.
17. _____ The nights are too cold.
18. _____ Dad goes on long walks.

FITNESS FLASH: Hop on your right foot for 30 seconds.

* See page 2.

DAY 17

Time/Writing

Use the calendars to answer each question.

May

S	M	T	W	Th	F	S
			1	2	3	4
5	6	7	8	9	10	11
12	13	14	15	16	17	18
19	20	21	22	23	24	25
26	27	28	29	30	31	

June

S	M	T	W	Th	F	S
						1
2	3	4	5	6	7	8
9	10	11	12	13	14	15
16	17	18	19	20	21	22
23	24	25	26	27	28	29
30						

1. Julia went to the dentist on the third Tuesday in May. What was the date?

   Tuesday, May _____

2. Heath started his dance class on the first Monday in June. What was the date?

   Monday, June _____

3. Today is May 10. Adam's family will see a play next Thursday. On what date will they see a play?

   Thursday, May _____

4. How many days are between May 29 and June 5?

   _____

What do you think would be the most difficult part about being a parent?

_____

_____

_____

CHARACTER CHECK: Discuss with an adult how long you think it takes to regain someone's trust after telling a lie.

Reading Comprehension

The Moon

The moon lights up the night sky. Sometimes, the moon looks narrow. Sometimes, it looks round. The appearance of the moon has to do with the position of the moon as viewed from Earth. When the moon is between the sun and Earth, the moon looks black. This is called a new moon. When Earth is between the sun and the moon, the moon looks bright and round. This is called a full moon. In the middle of these periods, half of the moon is lit, and half of the moon is dark. It takes about one month for the moon to finish the entire cycle.

1. What is the main idea of this passage?

    A. The moon can look thin or fat.

    B. The moon travels around Earth.

    C. The moon looks different throughout the month.

2. What makes the moon's appearance change? _____
   _____

3. When does a new moon happen? _____
   _____

4. What is the author's purpose for writing this passage?

    A. to tell facts about the moon's appearance

    B. to entertain the reader

    C. to encourage the reader to visit the moon

FACTOID: At least 26 rocks from Mars have landed on Earth.

DAY 19

Language Arts & Grammar/Place Value

Adverbs often answer the questions *where*, *when*, or *how*. Underline the adverb in each sentence. Then, circle *when*, *where*, or *how* to show what question it answers.

1. Mom and Dad clapped proudly for Shaun.   when   where   how
2. Yuki called Grandma yesterday.   when   where   how
3. Please take the puppy outside.   when   where   how
4. Will crossed the street safely.   when   where   how
5. Addy raced ahead of us.   when   where   how
6. I woke early to the chirps of birds.   when   where   how

Use the hundreds, tens, and ones blocks to help you solve each problem.

7. 343
   + 136
   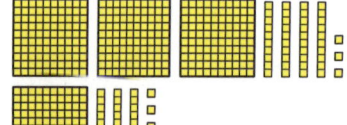

8. 542
   + 437
   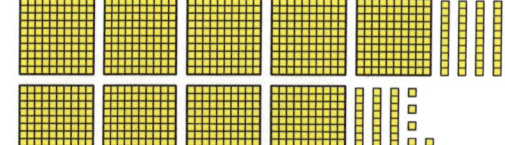

9. 698
   − 322
   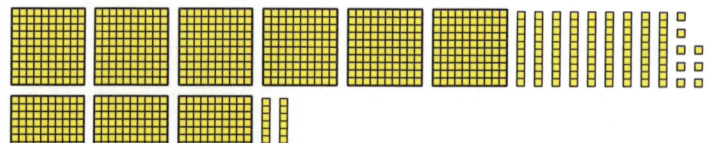

FACTOID: Some lungfish can survive out of the water for more than two years.

Science

Pinching Water

Can you hold two streams of water together? Can you separate two streams of water that had been flowing together? You would probably have to be pretty powerful! Or, would you?

Materials:
- nail (8- or 16-penny)
- hammer
- soup can (empty)
- water
- masking tape

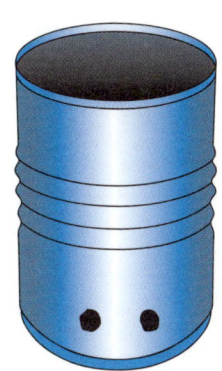

Procedure:
1. Ask an adult to use a hammer and nail to make two small holes in the lower section of the soup can. The holes should be close to the bottom and 0.5 inches (1.27 cm) apart. Tape over the holes.
2. Fill the can with water and hold it over a sink. Then, remove the tape.
3. Using your fingers, try to pinch the two streams of water together.
4. Using your fingers, try to split the two streams of water.

What's This All About?
When you pinch the streams of water together, the water molecules act like magnets. They attract each other and form larger water drops.

By splitting the water streams, you push the streams far enough away that they cannot attract each other. When this happens, they stay separate. As long as you have water in the can, you will be able to pinch or split the streams of water.

Take It Outside!

Outdoor Extension Activity

When you are outside, list the things you see, such as the names on your neighbors' mailboxes or street names. Practice putting the names in ABC order. As you improve, make the list longer to include many outside objects!

Word List

_____   _____

_____   _____

_____   _____

_____   _____

_____   _____

Now, challenge yourself to find something that starts with each letter of the alphabet. Good luck with *Q* and *X*!

A _____   J _____   S _____

B _____   K _____   T _____

C _____   L _____   U _____

D _____   M _____   V _____

E _____   N _____   W _____

F _____   O _____   X _____

G _____   P _____   Y _____

H _____   Q _____   Z _____

I _____   R _____

ANSWER KEY

Section I

Day 1/Page 6: The capital letters should be written from A to Z.; 1. o; 2. a; 3. e; 4. u; 5. i; 6. o

Day 2/Page 7: 1. 4; 2. 12; 3. 5; 4. 18; 5. 16; 6. 20; 7. 17; 8. 8; 9. 14; 10. 18; 11. 13; 12. 19

13. ;

14. ; 15. 6:30;

16. ; 17. 2:30;

18.

Day 3/Page 8: The lowercase letters should be written from a to z.; 1. Drawings will vary.

Day 4/Page 9: 1. Students should color one-half of the rectangle.; 2. Students should color one-fourth of the circle.; 3. Students should color two-fourths of the rectangle.; 4. 20; 5. 50; 6. 10; 7. 20; 8. 30; 9. 40

Day 5/Page 10:

Base Word	Add -ed	Add -ing
jump	jumped	jumping
pat	patted	patting
open	opened	opening
start	started	starting
touch	touched	touching
blink	blinked	blinking

1. e; 2. i; 3. o; 4. a; 5. a; 6. i

Day 6/Page 11: 1. 4; 2. 9; 3. 9; 4. 9; 5. 6; 6. 9; 7. 4; 8. 8; 9. 9; 10. 4; 11. 6; 12. 6; 13. 24; 14. 40; 15. 33; 16. 57; 17. 26; 18. 45

Day 8/Page 13: 1. Sanja ate soup for lunch.; 2. Eli will race down the hill.; 3. Abby splashes her brother in the pool.; 4. The piano needs to be tuned.; 5. o; 6. u; 7. a; 8. e; 9. a; 10. i

Day 9/Page 14: 1. 14; 2. 9; 3. 10; 4. 1; 5. 18; 6. 2; 7. dr; 8. tr; 9. gr; 10. cl; 11. gl; 12. st

Day 11/Page 18: 1. 19, 39; 2. 80, 100; 3. 3, 23; 4. 65, 85; 5. Ducks like to swim.; 6. Can we play in the sandbox?; 7. Some birds make nests in trees.; 8. Are you having fun today?

Day 12/Page 19: 1. 9, 9, 4, 5; 2. 2, 6, 8, 6, 2, 6; 3. Answers will vary but may include: 7, 3, 10, 3, 7, 10, 10, 7, 3, 10, 3, 7;

Common Nouns	Proper Nouns
hippo	Olivia
holiday	Greenlawn Library
cousin	Dr. Yang
store	Thanksgiving

Day 13/Page 20: 1. Q; 2. E; 3. C; 4. S; 5. S; 6. and; 7. or; 8. so; 9. but

Day 14/Page 21: 1. Bella's balloon; 2. Kate's kite; 3. Hasaan's hat; 4. Sammy's soccer ball; 5. 2; 6. 1; 7. 1; 8. 2

Day 15/Page 22: 1. 4, 1; 2. 4, 5; 3. 8, 4; 4. 6, 5; 5. 7, 2; 6. 1, 7; 7. 3, 9; 8. 5, 0; 9. 5, 1; 10. 9, 7; 11. 10, 0; Answers will vary.

Day 17/Page 24: 1. <; 2. >; 3. <; 4. >; 5. >; 6. >; 7. >; 8. <; 9. <; 10. <; 11. >; 12. >; 13. <; 14. <; 15. >; 16. 4; 17. 2; 18. 5; 19. 3; 20. 1

Day 18/Page 25:

1. ; 2. 4:00;

3. ; 4. 11:00;

5. ; 6. 8:30;

7. ch; 8. wh; 9. sh

Day 19/Page 26: 1. 1; 2. 3; 3. 2; 4. C; 5. A; 6. B

Section II

Day 1/Page 30: 1. 65, 80, 85; 2. 330, 360, 380; 3. 500, 600, 800; 4.–5. Answers will vary.

Day 2/Page 31: 1. 154; 2. 90; 3. 122; 4. 75; 5. glue; 6. frog; 7. clock; 8. bowl

ANSWER KEY

Day 3/Page 32: 1. C; 2. B; 3. it is; 4. we are; 5. you have; 6. do not; 7. we will; 8. is not

Day 5/Page 34: 1. 48¢; 2. 62¢; 3. 39¢; 4. 25¢; 5. 12; 6. 12; 7. 10; 8. 14; 9. 17; 10. 16; 11. 4; 12. 5; 13. 4; 14. 0; 15. 8; 16. 14

Day 6/Page 35: 1. sipped; 2. pounded; 3. nervous; 4. exhausted; 5. 12, even; 6. 18, even; 7. 9, odd; 8. 5, odd

Day 7/Page 36:

Long a	Long e	Long i
apron	eagle	rider
Monday	season	bedtime
flavor	fever	unkind

Long o	Long u
frozen	bugle
ocean	argue
hello	human

1. you; 2. give; 3. sit; 4. mix

Day 9/Page 38: Answers will vary.; Answers will vary.

Day 10/Page 39:

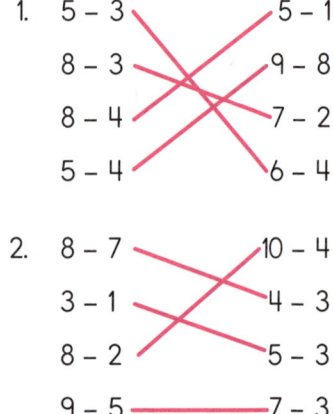

3.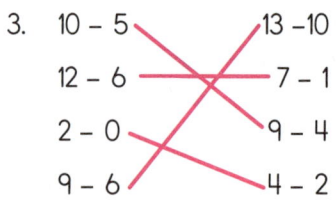

4.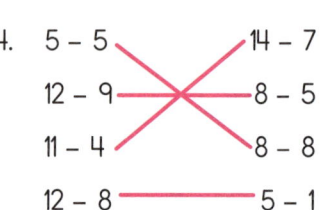

5. gift, his; 6. car, flat; 7. sat, the; 8. dad, store

Day 11/Page 42: 1. e, i, e, e, i; 2. i, e, i, e, e; 3. i, i, e, e, i; children; mice; foot; men; tooth; person

Day 12/Page 43: 1. 53; 2. 97; 3. 30; 4. 57; 5. 78; 6. 79; 7. 8, 10, 12; 8. 10, 20, 25;

Day 13/Page 44: 1. Students should divide rectangle into 3 rows and 4 columns, 12.; 2. Students should divide rectangle into 4 rows and 5 columns, 20.; 3. boy, shoe; 4. She, letter, aunt; 5. you, sandwich; 6. We, movie, butterflies; 7. sister, ring

Day 14/Page 45: 1. gold/fish; 2. pop/corn; 3. day/time; 4. dog/house; 5. space/ship; 6. rail/road; 7. blue/berry; 8. sail/boat; 9. grape/fruit; 10. cup/cake; 11. news/paper; 12. some/time; 13. 2; 14. 3; 15. 4; 16. 1

Day 15/Page 46: 1. 1, 0, 1; 2. 1, 4, 3; 3. 1, 9, 11; 4. 9, 3, 2; 5. can't; 6. I'm; 7. you're; 8. don't; 9. he's; 10. I'll; 11. did not; 12. is not; 13. you have; 14. she is; 15. could not; 16. we are

Day 16/Page 47: 1. are; 2. is; 3. is; 4. are; 5. Is; 6. Are; Answers will vary.; Answers will vary.; 7. ?; 8. !; 9. !; 10. ?; 11. .

Day 18/Page 49: 1. Students should underline three times the v and d in valentine's day.; 2. Students should underline three times the t and c in tasty crunch.; 3. Students should underline three times the l and d in labor day.; 4. Students should underline three times the c and n in chicken nibblers.; 5. ourselves; 6. themselves; 7. yourself; 8. herself; 9. myself

Day 20/Page 51: 1. Two nickels should be circled.; 2. A penny, a nickel, and a dime should be circled.; 3. Two dimes and a nickel should be circled.; 4. Four dimes and a nickel should be circled.; 5. not safe; 6. build again; 7. not like; 8. cook before

Section III

Day 1/Page 54: 1. Jackson made a fruit salad, and Lena brought dessert.; 2. The bunny hopped across the yard, but the cat did not see it.; 3. I could hear the rain on the roof, so I knew the storm had begun.; 4. Julia walks to school with Chase, or she rides the bus.; 5. can't; 6. easy; 7. key; 8. buy; 9. light; 10. once; 11. carry; 12. you're; 13. star; 14. funny

Day 2/Page 55: 1. 9 miles; 2. 9 miles; 3. no; 4. no; 5. yes; 6. no; 7. yes; 8. no; 9. no

Day 3/Page 56: 1. 41; 2. 71; 3. 93; 4. 81; 5. 100; 6. 100; 7. 27; 8. 63; 9. 67; 10. 26; 11. 29; 12. 17; 13. 9 cm, 6 cm, 3 cm; 14. 8 cm, 4 cm, 4 cm

Day 4/Page 57: 1. 996; 2. 21; 3. 82; 4. 37; 5. 265; 6. 661; 7. 79; 8. 58; 9. 22; 10. 780; 11. 118; 12. 100; 13. 46 inches; 14. 58 sunflowers; 15. 92 cans; 16. $18

Day 5/Page 58: 1. 55 students; 2. 91 shells; 3. 32 laps; 4. 84 fish; 5. B, C

Day 7/Page 60: 1. A; 2. E; 3. F; 4. C; 5. B; 6. D; Answers will vary.

Day 9/Page 62: 1. wash the car; 2. $7.00; 3. $0.50; 4. N; 5. Y; 6. Y; 7. N; 8. Y; 9. N; 10. Y; 11. N

Day 10/Page 63: 1. Three-fourths of the shape should be colored.; 2. One-third of the shape should be colored.; 3. One-fourth of the shape should be colored.; 4. Two-thirds of the shape should be colored.; 5. fruit bowls; 6. 20 more fruit bowls; 7. fruit bowls

Day 11/Page 66: 1. 12:00; 2. 9:15; 3. 2:30; 4. 4:00; 5. a/part/ment; 6. e/nor/mous; 7. sub/trac/tion; 8. won/der/ful

Day 12/Page 67: 1. 10, 12, 14, 16, 18, 20, +2; 2. 20, 25, 30, 35, 40, 45, +5; 3. 15, 18, 21, 24, 27, 30, +3; 4. table; 5. square; 6. sky; 7. light

Day 13/Page 68: 1. 9; 2. 6; 3. 12; 4. 15; 5. 12; 6. 8; 7. 20; 8. 16; 9. to change from a liquid into a gas; 10. camouflage; 11. dry; 12. Possible answers: rain and snow

Day 15/Page 70: 1. 3, 4, 1, 300 + 40 + 1; 2. 5, 6, 3, 500 + 60 + 3; 3. 7, 5, 2, 700 + 50 + 2; 4. 8, 4, 5, 800 + 40 + 5; 5. 65; 6. 74; 7. 30

Day 16/Page 71: 1. <; 2. >; 3. >; 4. <; 5. <; 6. >; 7. <; 8. <; 9. <; 10. >; 11. >; 12. <; 13. O; 14. F; 15. F; 16. O; 17. O; 18. O

Day 17/Page 72: 1. 21; 2. 3; 3. 16; 4. 6; Answers will vary.

Day 18/Page 73: 1. C; 2. The position of the moon as viewed from Earth makes the moon's appearance change.; 3. A new moon happens when the moon is between the sun and the earth.; 4. A

Day 19/Page 74: 1. proudly, how; 2. yesterday, when; 3. outside, where; 4. safely, how; 5. ahead, where; 6. early, when; 7. 479; 8. 979; 9. 376

NOTES